DOPAMINE AND THE DEVIL

MATTHEW FREEMAN

Kenmore, WA

A Coffeetown Press book published by Epicenter Press

Epicenter Press
6524 NE 181st St.
Suite 2
Kenmore, WA 98028

For more information go to:
www.Camelpress.com
www.Coffeetownpress.com
www.Epicenterpress.com
@FreemanPoet on X and BlueSky; Matthew Scott Freeman on Facebook

All rights reserved. No part of this book may be reproduced or transmitted in any form or by any means, electronic or mechanical, including photocopying, recording, or any information storage and retrieval system, without permission in writing from the publisher.

This is a work of fiction. Names, characters, places, brands, media, and incidents are either the product of the author's imagination or are used fictitiously.

Cover illustration by Dane Marti
Cover design by Scott Book
Design by Melissa Vail Coffman

Dopamine and the Devil
Copyright © 2025 by Matthew Freeman

Library of Congress Control Number: 2025937023

ISBN: 978-1-68492-264-2 (Trade Paper)
ISBN: 978-1-68492-265-9 (eBook)

For Nolen and Lodes

CONTENTS

Looking Down as I Walk 1
Prescription Authority 2
Ex Experientia 3
Driven Out 4
Maybe It's Just Me 5
I Used to be Possessed 6
Same Old Same Old 7
Choose Your Words Carefully 8
Motomart Fancy 9
Back to the Prelude 10
After the Prelude 11
A Very Low Percentage 12
I Catch a Break 13
Total Insight 14
What I Told Starla 15
Update 16
Structure Everywhere 17
The Historical Gesture 18
A Celebration 19
Start From Nothing Means Anything and Proceed 20

My First Ever Insight 21
A Plain Matter of Fact. 22
Messed Up 23
New Life on the Mississippi 24
Portentous Dispensary 25
From Destitution to the Branding 26
Columbia Crown: Ten Sentences 27
Consolation Clear 37
Wrong Places 38
Canon 39
The Spirit is With Me 40
Rich Producer 42
Given 43
My Heroes Were All Dead by Now 44
Letting Go in Carbondale 45
Works Are Dead 46
Nullified 47
Happenstance on Dale Ave. 48
Contrary 49
Just a Kid From Missouri 50
Problems 51
Gracious 52
Another Life 53
A Good Fit 54
Refresh 55
My Charm 59
Hot Eggs 60
A Plea 61
Toothpaste 63
Who I Am 64
Rondo 65

The Victor	66
My Briefest Brief	67
Hearing Back	68
A Demon!	69
For Kaye	70
A Bit of Alchemy	71
A Lamb	72
Bobby	73
Counter Sublime?	74
A Little Innocent	75
So That Maybe I'm Still In the Game	76
It's Weird the Way Things Turn Out	77
Granted	78
Damning	79
Tired	80
Thanks	81
Dissipation	82
Small	83
It Wasn't Me	84
It Ends With the Devil	85
I Appropriate the Literal	86
An Incomplete Conclusion to the Evil Pestilence	88
Just Following	89
I Dare Say	90
Spent	91
Measured	92
iPod, Diet Dr Pepper, Cigarette	93
No Doubt	94
Into Himself	95
Stands For Something Else	96
Technology Freakout	97

What's to Love	98
Taxed	99
Grandma Ruth Planting Flowers	100
Drop the Microphone Scenario	101
Forget Whitman	102
Novel	103
Wallet So Slim	104
Popsicle Sticks	106
The Sweet Theorist at SLU	107
Bomb	108
Sense	109
Mouthing Off to My Analyst and Then Apologizing	110
Starting Again	111
Oh, the Complications Psychosis Causes	112
Freeman Strikes Again	113
Spotting It	114
Some Kind	115
What?	116
My Year	117
An Explanation	118
Having Paid Attention in Math Class	120
Their World	121
Some Import to Names	122
More Heresy	123
My Dreams	124
Between Analysis	126
Is That Irony	127
Forever	128
My Friends, the Short Version	129

ACKNOWLEDGMENTS

Grateful acknowledgment is made to 2River, who published many of these poems in a chapbook called *Exile*.

Grateful acknowledgment is made to the journals in which many of these poems appeared: Alien Buddha, Anti-heroin Chic, Blue Mountain Review, Neuro Logical, Cerasus Magazine, Gutslut Press, Fevers of the Mind, and The Blood Pudding.

> Wish the bliss
>   could never take flight
>   — Q-Tip

LOOKING DOWN AS I WALK

The life of the mind
is writing your name
on a jailhouse wall.

I guess I had to go to hell.
And now the stupid bell rings
when I walk by Richmond Place
and it freaks me out like it always did
as I recall how Michele
had warned me when I was on
the precipice of solipsism.

But like I said, I had to go.
And if there'd been some hand
to hold in that
drastic symbolic mess
I would have grasped it.

PRESCRIPTION AUTHORITY

You would do well
to remind yourself
of all those times walking around
and thinking,
"I need help."

Because now
when you're at the family reunion
they're all like,
"Matt's the one with the diagnosis
but he's the sanest of us all."

You would do well
to figure out
how that happened.

EX EXPERIENTIA

There's a squirrel rooting around in the trash
and of course I'm lucky to be alive
having fallen off
so many elegant balustrades
and stolen expensive bottles of wine
at parties to which I was not invited
and how many times
have the cops let me off with a warning
and how many times
have I tackled a trash can
and then late night walked down Grand
over the old railroad tracks
when I wanted to experience everything
like the tide rips up in Alaska knitting
or wake to mountains so clear in Colorado
under a flimsy sleeping bag
only to be drawn out of nature
with some medical condition
and I have hung with pink fingers
off the top floor of the parking garage
across from the old Busch Stadium
saying the same thing over and over but a bit
differently as when very drunk at Humphries on a
Sunday the mid-morning light coming in I walked
across the street and went up to the deserted
English department after so many drop-outs and
expulsions and could faintly hear someone laughing.

DRIVEN OUT

I'm just dumb enough
to believe
in the resurrection.

And all of that aggression, and
every ounce of the horrible dark drive
has been driven out of me.

I love that I can see things
two ways. I'm the lucky one.
I knew guys
in the hospital
who were never, never coming back.
One had long yellow fingernails
and a trembling hand
and would ask under his breath
if anyone had shorts, meaning
the last little bit of a cigarette.
One had a dirty page out of a notebook
with wild scrawl listing the names
of her fifty sons. All the names
were oddly similar and if you
challenged her in any way she would scream.

For a long time, I was one. And then some
maverick doctor put me on three heavy
antipsychotics at once. I consider it a miracle.

MAYBE IT'S JUST ME

Last night in the wee hours I opened
a book of poems by
a very old and wise woman
and I found the poems to be
sublime and awful, all interwoven
and suggestive. In short,
I was afraid. And then this morning
before I closed the book
the poems were clear and concise, almost classical.

I am taking a walk down Freeman Street
to where it dead-ends creepily
into a forest with a little trail.
As I go along I find an even smaller trail
jutting off and I take that one
and when I get to the edge of the creek
there's a clearing with a little circle
of Stonehenge-type stones
and an altar in the middle with feathers on it.
I don't know what kind of shit this is
but I do know that
I never wanted to have power over anyone.

And I know that I have been
in a battle for the soul, and that I
have messed the devil up, and that I have died
and come back. I am sorry that men are destroying the world.

I USED TO BE POSSESSED

It's a terrifying thing to find
your voice in this world.
In the moment
God seizes you by the legs
as you walk through Babylon
on a sultry night
in the Loop
and not one image of the plague
gets through to you.

This is hard. Oh, I fought the devil—
I was really
making fun of him
and after every jest he put
this punishing pulse through my brain.

As I've gone along, the doubt
about my secret mission
has begun to dissipate.
I'm learning things I knew
when I first started out.

I could never write a sermon.
And I certainly could never write
an essay about whatever went down
in Dogtown. But I can walk into the woods
and come to this dense creepy part where
there's an altar and my eyes light up: No Vacancy.

SAME OLD SAME OLD

We were going to study the High Romantics
in high school
and on the first day of class
our teacher asked—and this was
the teacher I'd visit in a couple of years
at two in the morning
drunk with my scribblings—
"What does it take for a civilization to produce poetry?"
We were all nonplussed and quiet.
"FREE TIME," came his answer.

And so because of some wretchedness I must endure
I get a modest check from
the government and am able to remain
very fanciful. I didn't plan this out.
Back when I was first in the hospital
and thought Level Three
meant you kissed three nurses,
believe me, I had no idea there was any money in this.
I feel pretty guilty still
that I was able to come home
and put on about three pots of coffee a day
and pace back and forth while everyone worked
and talk to myself and write poetry.
As for my teachers, now we're friends on Facebook. As for me,
I'm trying so hard to not burn any holes
in the beautiful new Dockers my sister bought me.

CHOOSE YOUR WORDS CAREFULLY

Well, I've earned it. Whatever this is.
Not in the usual way,
of course. I earned it
by lying in bed in Columbia and
tripping my ass off and writhing.

The best thing
that could have happened to me
was missing a dose
of my heart medicine.
I was walking around
this beautiful silent neighborhood
in a weird panic
when I just had to realize
that I would be subject to
a constant low-grade anxiety
even if I took my thirteen meds.
We call that "acceptance," Chief said.

It's another of my myriad amusings
on why I'm alone. I have defeated
the devil all over again
but the process messed
up my imagination and now
I have no relation to reality.
I accidentally made an innuendo
and the sparrow flew.

MOTOMART FANCY

Whenever we would cruise
down Route 3 on our way
to Waterloo where we could party
without anyone
knowing us in Chief's deceased
grandma's house

I always had horrible visions
of standing broke down
on the side of the road stoned and breathless
without any money and out of options
and having no reprieve
in the bitter gravel
while the Ideal Spirit was all around me

and once we stopped for gas at the Motomart
and Chief gave me some money
for Michelob and the cashier in there
was like a high school kid with zits.
"You look really young," he said to me.

My God, I said to Chief. That kid was into me!
And he thought I was a vampire and wanted
to be a vampire too. He's gonna find out where
we're staying and get us into an orgy. His friends
are gonna do meth in your grandma's house!
Settle down, said Chief. It's only Intellectual Beauty.

BACK TO THE PRELUDE

I am locked in now, hardstyle,
and I can only write
about one thing. And that
would be the effort to get to the crest
and then fall apart.

After sitting all night between
the calm disturbed young woman
and the nervous disturbed young man
I started to come out of the catatonia
as the fluorescent lights came up
and people started gathering
for vitals and breakfast. My mind
was still behaving as if it were
an ocean.

Suddenly a very old woman wheeled
up and took my hand and we looked
into each other's eyes
and we were secretly satisfied
without ever moving our mouths
and in the back I heard "The Change" and "Orgy"
and I got a little away from myself
there as I kept trying to escape.

I guess I won't quit writing about
secrets and psychosis, my
autobiography of decay. I know why some
people sit still all day looking at nothing.

AFTER THE PRELUDE

Hardstyle is hearing
the nurses in the next room
calling you to a terrifying orgy
and having
no idea whether what
you're hearing is half-baked
or ingenuous.

After twenty years all I have to
deal with are the
embers of my once hot head.
There was some half life decay
on the other side
of that elegant door.

You can't find any hatred here or happenstance
in the dark room with the big TV
and if I do Hotmail and stay apart
and say my prayer it's always the case
that God let's me off the hook.
I'm chronic.

A VERY LOW PERCENTAGE

He was an academic poet
who wasn't allowed anywhere
near the academy.

And he wasn't bitter. No, he was
never bitter. He
walked around in every kind of weather
and wherever he went he felt
that he was the luckiest guy in the world.

He had something going on
with his heart, his hair
was thinning and he had fake teeth,
he had to give himself an insulin shot
and he took all kinds of psych meds
and while he was alone all the time
he never felt lonely.

He had gone through total insanity
and come out nearly clear and clean
on the other side
and he could see things two ways
and marvel at Time
and stand in awe at the Presence
and really, really,
how many people could say that?

I CATCH A BREAK

Evidently the guy who
helps out people in distress
and gives a few cigarettes
and a couple of bucks to the homeless
is a total illusion created
by the Big Other.

After thirty years of this shit
I've found the unknown
is simply
a couple of declarative sentences.

Back when I was trying
to facilitate my fictional status
and Das Man was so merciful in telling me
to go ahead and write my poems I became unmoored
and walked into
a party on the highest floor of Scholars House
and pounded a bottle and exclaimed
in the polite silence, "This wine sucks!"

I'd relinquish everything to the void
but there ain't no void
when God is with us. Believe me,
I didn't just make up a bunch of shit.

TOTAL INSIGHT

It's like you take a loving gesture
from your brilliant
mentor and friend, something under his breath,
and you turn it through,
you turn it into something sinister
and the smile becomes a mocking smile,
and you sadly realize you're immortal.
And your analyst has a field day with "You."

But I will say this:
If you make aggressive dance moves
close to me while I'm trying to drink my coffee
then later that night at the bar
you and your scraggily buddy
are going to be bounced
and I'm going to see it happen
while I casually sip my Diet Coke
as I sit next to
my beautiful social worker friend.

WHAT I TOLD STARLA

I've achieved a new level. Now I'm
even a part of the Master Discourse!

Out in the foyer sitting across from me
was a woman waiting for a ride to church
and you could tell from her body language,
like the way she kept moving her foot,
that she was either trying to hypnotize me
or get me to match her breathing

but I was so relaxed and natural—
I could move my hands any way I wanted
and I didn't have to worry about
any wayward influence, I could even
speak if I felt like it. Now I can speak!

Well, I'm still learning stuff. I think
if I ever got hospitalized again
I'd do pretty well with the ladies. When
I discovered I had a misshapen mind the true
work of communication began. No wonder
there's a soul that precipitates such eloquence.
I'm coming down off a horrible trip and
trying to apply the secrets. After sitting quietly
for ten minutes the woman in the foyer was like,
"Are you waiting for someone?"

UPDATE

You have to simply let go of the idea
that things are going to
make sense. The pharmakon
is the cop on the line after you've lost service,
after you've bought a dime bag on Main Street.
Dude, I'm talking about a really big presence.

You've got to deal with the fluctuations,
doing Latin conjugations at two in the morn
while everybody is loudly listening
to heavy metal and doing coke
and referring to you and you can't stop
thinking about the really cool
woman therapist at the bar who said
you were more interesting
than your rich muscle-bound crazy buddy.
But all that was just your education.

It's only time, the teleological con artist
who's really made of concentric circles
and whose construct is so fleeting.
Anyhow, that's what I put in my alumni notes.

STRUCTURE EVERYWHERE

I've disabled Das Man! I dismantled
him in a ten-year analytic undoing.
His voice now is so small, so
obsequious, sad.
But I still love my denatured dad.
And when I see someone
I'd like to date
I don't feel so horrible and bad.

I keep having this dream where I'm upstairs
in my parents' house and I'm cleaning out
all the old books and dirty VHS tapes and dusty pictures
and today I woke up and
took an early dose of Ativan and met a new friend
and felt almost like I did when I was a kid,
that everything was going to be clear.

Listen: if they don't take your vitals anymore
in the morning at MPC it's because of me. I'm in
a class with Foucault eagerly, eagerly raising my hand.
Jakob Dylan wrote me a song. That's reasonable.
And I know now I'm not going
to be left out to die in the wind and the snow.
I've got the capacity for metaphor!
That's just one more reminder that everything's connected.

THE HISTORICAL GESTURE

I was just a suffering little bird
who was learning to sing
when I kept getting called
into the counselor's office on Monday morning
and asked to explain
all the shit I did over the weekend.

Oh, I was just reading the High Romantics.
Well, maybe a cop made me pour out all my beer.

I was expelled and asked to return,
like the truest of pharmakons, so desiccated
and wrapped up so tight
in my own consciousness I couldn't see
that everyone wanted to make love to me.
Chief had turned me onto Morrissey a little too early.
Someone predicted I'd end up on the streets.

It's the Missouri Synod, they've completely
displaced the Greek; don't you think
the Jesuit who keeps a little booze in his desk
is a little more ambiguous? You can't get any
information anymore. Is there a war on? What
does each side believe? I'm leaving this mendacity.
This is exactly what the devil wanted.

A CELEBRATION

I've experienced the greatest insight
I've ever had! Now everything makes sense,
everything has come together,
you could even say
I've gone through another huge cathexis.
Somehow God let me look at my illness.
I don't know how it happened, I can't begin to explain it,
but I was sitting in my chair
confused and distraught as ever,
when suddenly I looked into the distance
and actually saw schizophrenia
and something simple in my consciousness clicked.
I don't have all these myriad
symptoms that don't make any sense.
There's just this concrete electric vibe
and the in-trouble criminal feeling
that connects the anxiety and paranoia and sorrow
and numbness and anhedonia and timidity and old voices
and fear and desperation to please and worry
about the end of the world. Now I know
how clean I am, and why
schizophrenia didn't come until I was writing poems
when I was coming off
what I thought at the time was a normal childhood
full of good grades and shyness and sports and presence.
Oh, we can still call it the devil,
we can call it whatever we want!
But my mission is clear and I'm clearly rooted,
maybe I'll even sing in the shower again,
maybe I'll listen to the old Irish songs and get sad,
maybe I'll make a joke,
maybe I'll let the necromedia gently fall away and croak.

START FROM NOTHING MEANS ANYTHING AND PROCEED

So, we've witnessed the death
of the signified. And every day
the necromedia comes out
with a new batch of noise.
My grand narrative was going to be
I was a good kid and got
schizophrenia and ended up in the poor house
and blossomed. But to see correctly
you've got to get completely free of nonsense.

My cousin thinks I ought to move to Portland.
Well, maybe I'm in Portland right now.
When I was sleeping everything changed.
I'm famous at last! Five or ten
people know who I am. When I rise
the first thing I'm going to do
is go to the emergency room
and demand a spinal tap.

I'm smoking a cigarette in the drizzling rain
and wondering about Diana
and the rain is messed up and the wind is messed up
and the trees and the bees are messed up
and I remember waiting for the sun to rise
outside Diana's friend's mansion when we were young
with nothing to do but exist
and smell like sex.

MY FIRST EVER INSIGHT

It was a bird talking. And I
was supposed to be on another

level, one where people communicated
and everything would be revealed to me.

After they let me race around the women's
ward I was called into the conference room

to be interviewed by six shrinks
and I went in smirking and intense

and declared I'd found my object relation
and the secret local newscaster they had sitting in

deliberately tapped her toe and one doctor
asked if I could fly and I said I felt like

jumping out the window and taking off into the sky
but that wasn't physically possible and he said

that's a good start and I felt like a toddler again
going from the pure illusion of love into

the gnosis of the body of light. Write your obsessions,
they say. I say lay down your miracles.

A PLAIN MATTER OF FACT

When I was going through the
change down in Columbia, Missouri
I'd claimed
I was allergic to Haldol

so these assholes at Mid-Mo
put me on Navane
which was even worse

and you had to stand at the sink
with the water running
in order
to trick yourself into pissing

and Level Three
meant you kissed three nurses
and I found out I was a vampire
and they'd taped comics to the wall
to teach me structure

as I fell into the function of the unreal
and became immersed in communion
and my shrink was like this
is really important Matt have you taken
any drugs and I was like I got high two weeks ago
with my Latin TA and he sang to me Jesus' own
declension.

MESSED UP

I'm getting a really strange concoction
of peace and anxiety here.
I'm wondering again about St Paul in Rome.
This Reality that's thrust upon me—
I'm only praying that it's benign.
Like when I was chasing my dad
around the dirty living room
with a tattered Bible, screaming,
someday we'll laugh about all of this.

Now the old bards are calling me
away from the blogs and I recall
mixing up language in my mom's basement
when something funny
was going on with electricity
and I was shattered
after taking some of my older sister's Zoloft
she'd left in the medicine cabinet

and here I come meaning words get all messed up
with the weight of what they call
the world breaking apart
and it's really not too complicated
to sit solo at the bar in Blueberry Hill
and pick up the bartender's semaphores
under the ritual of multiple Diet Cokes.

NEW LIFE ON THE MISSISSIPPI

I have this old safe
that's full of my poems
but last night I dreamt
that it was full of
little nuclear missiles.

I looked and looked
for someone in authority
to tell about it
but when I found her
she didn't want to hear me.
"At least let me give you
the combination," I said.
"That way I'll feel free."

She sent me
to the nearest advertising
agency and I started
drinking again and
making all kinds of money.
One night, working late,
I stood at the window.
Our building was situated
right in the middle
of the Poplar Street Bridge.
It was dark,
but I was able to see
that the Muddy Mississippi
was now full
of bright colorful Skittles.

PORTENTOUS DISPENSARY

When Ladylove took me back
to Carbondale for Christmas
the first thing we did
was hit the dispensary
and when they took him into
the inner sanctum
I was left out
with the receptionist and the security guard
and everything was quiet and charged
when suddenly the receptionist said,
"Order for Matthew 'Cross'" and
she and the guard were just cracking up
and I was so still and
she then said "I just had to do it"
and I knew right then
light as hell
it was going to be my annus mirabilis
because I had outlived
all of my influences
and time was up
and I saw clearly through some kind of screen
and then Ladylove came out
with the dope
and we split.

FROM DESTITUTION TO THE BRANDING

I was wide awake, standing
at the dry erase board
next to the occupational therapist
when he said,
"So you're not a vampire anymore?"
"A vampire!" I exclaimed.
"Dude, I'm a Christian."
"Oh, here we go," he said.

And I don't know what you want me to say here,
that I was alone,
that I experienced some type of emotion,
that I had been through so much trauma,
that I thought I was dying and couldn't talk to anyone,
or how about how it's years later and
I was just sitting in the parking lot
cross-legged in the cold
with my smoke and my iPod and my Diet Dr Pepper
and Stan came by to say
that I looked like some kind of beggar
and I easily laughed and said
no I'm like Marlowe telling his story on the Thames.
I don't think Stan got the reference.
It doesn't matter. This is an ad for Diet Dr Pepper.

COLUMBIA CROWN: TEN SENTENCES

Back towards the tail end of my trying
as I was making my last gasp at Mizzou
I slowly began to notice
that when the autumn leaves were coming
down the usual
beautifully sad feeling didn't wash over me
and the wind and the rain
left me nothing but numb
and I walked to class with a burning
guilt over having flunked out
of the most lenient school in the land
and I was weary and determined
to finish my degree at the incredibly old
age of twenty-three and something was off.

As I walked down Anthony Street
from my room in the
old beautiful sad house that I could
clearly see and not perceive
it occurred to me that in my backpack
was the thick Abnormal Psychology textbook
that I had recently bought
embarrassed and sweating in the bookstore
among kids who were supposed to be there
and wouldn't it be sweet to sit and skip class
in the leaves and the grass by
the apartment complex and pore over the pages
and find my problem but every word was foreign
and I found no delight there, forlorn without affect.

I noticed a kid in Latin class who had
shaggy hair and wanted to be a lawyer
and his whole demeanor was calm and pleasing
and he smoked a lot of weed Oh that must be
what it is so I approached
the dealer as he drove by on Anthony
and nervously bought some marijuana
while a young woman from Structuralism
walked by suspiciously and I went
upstairs and lit myself on fire and felt
nature decay there drooping dead in the
beautiful dusty old house and words
got screwed up and I picked up the phone
and a police officer apologized for being on the line.

I was out one night in the rain
taking my original walk of shame
when crossing the street
became utterly impossible
and my heart was beating like a soughed bell
and I tried to go into the computer lab
but turned around and found
myself outside the emergency room
cupping my hand over my cigarette
like JFK and James Dean would do
whose names as they came up mocked me
and a casual nurse came out to smoke
beneath the overhang and asked
me how long it had been raining and I made
my first big revelation: Time is tricky.

I was curious so I walked to my cousin's
apartment and it seemed as if
the forest on the way was full of terrifying orgies
so I asked a power-walker to call the police
and then my cousin grabbed my shoulder
and took me in and told me to talk to my sister
but when I got on the phone I heard the devil
and threw the phone and screamed
and my cousin drove me to the hospital
and I waited in the running car as he went in
and I knew nothing could stop me
from driving off in his car and going far away
maybe up to Chicago where my sister lived and
talk to her roommate but then they came and got me.

I kept trying to escape from the hospital in part
because they were trying to make my room
look like my room in the old house on Anthony
and in part because something was happening
with language and in part because the therapist
had said ". . .in order for you to get out of here. . ." to
a large group of patients and in part because
Jakob Dylan was on the cover of a magazine
saying, "It's not so difficult, Matt," and then
a young patient looked at me
and when her mother visited they gave me
some KFC and her mother asked if she could
anoint me and as the hot oil cascaded over my hair
I was caught up there guilty and implicated.

It was terrible
to come back to Saint Anthony Street
and see the pages of the books I'd ripped apart
and feel the cold wind coming from the
broken window and read
the wild treatise I'd written
on the primary process and Martin Luther
and somewhat clear and nervous
to sadly return to class
with only a threadbare notebook and cheap pen
and hear so many scary words echoing
like schizophrenia and psychotic break
and religious ideation, to carry those
words around and to leave class early.

I was back in my Father's house
writing songs in the basement
and making creepy phone calls
to friends I hadn't seen in years
and I was on three antipsychotics at once
and putting on so much weight
because my intuition said eat
and what could I do but follow my intuition
and there was still a crack
in the sliding glass doors from when
I had shot off my BB gun as a kid
and that was so remote there were
cobwebs everywhere now and dead meat
in the broken freezer and I could not leave.

I lay dreaming of the hospital
and again something came up missing
because I had left too soon crying
on the phone for my mom
to come and get me and sign me out
before they could raise me
and the guy who thought he was a vampire
or I was a vampire because
when they took my blood they failed
to put a band-aid on and then
they'd let me have the run of the ward
when I first came in and then separated
me and eased me into group therapy
but I couldn't sit still and frenetically made the call.

And I remembered sad beautiful and numb
in Structuralism when Mary told me
about an open mic that night
and said "You need to go" and how
the gorgeous hunk said Matt just because
something's true for you
doesn't mean it's true for me
and then Mary said she saw a therapist
and walked in and immediately cried
and I said I can't cry bad things
keep happening but I just can't cry
and I tried to leave class then but Mary
took me by the arm and brought me back because
there was still something I needed to decipher.

CONSOLATION CLEAR

"Would they have medicated Jesus Christ?"
I asked my uncle, severe intellect,
when I had just come from the hospital.
"But Jesus Christ was not delusional,"
my uncle said. "He was a son of God."

How off had been my thinking, I reflect,
who never rose or ever moved a boulder.
My uncle passed, I got a little older
and grew to miss the clarity he wove,
and when I strove with demons in a dream,
I felt him put his arm around my shoulder.

WRONG PLACES

The disorganization of the senses
is recurring quite gently
and naturally. Sometimes I find myself
in the middle of the night
locked out of my room with no shirt on.
I have to sleep on the couch in the basement
until the maintenance guys come.
It's really a great big allegory.

Then the old criminal feeling comes back
to connive me into sorrow
as Bruckner says Let's get a drink
and I argue that I'm a raging alcoholic
and he says Oh you'll drink again
and the flowers in my room are fake
and the clock is going wild
and here:

Hellhounds are on my tail.
And that's a statement completely outside
of the medical discourse. I wonder what
a cognitive behavioralist would make of it.
They couldn't tell me to turn my demons into angels.
They have no method of incorporating such *parole*.
Maybe I need to consult a blues singer.
Maybe I've been hanging out in all the wrong places.

CANON

Why suffer so much,
why feel so freaked out and down
and consigned
to silence

and do everything in a rigid uptight time-set
and rapacious judgment coming down

when you can break it down to dopamine
or even the devil with his numb dead presence—
or what about what went down
in Dogtown when you were raised?

THE SPIRIT IS WITH ME

You smoked some dope and that's the devil
or it changed your brain chemistry
because you were sixteen
or you smoked some dope and it opened a door
or your dad was possessed by a demon
or you read about Alastair Crowley
or you smoked some dope and thought you were in love
and you were in love and all confused
and smoked some dope at a party
you banged your head really hard on a door
and your dad had PTSD from Vietnam
but your mom and dad smoked dope at a party
on the night you were conceived
and let a demon in
so you have chronic undifferentiated schizophrenia
so you will be possessed by the devil forever
so when you die you'll go to hell not because
of the shit you did or the dope you smoked
but just because you're on such a bad trip
you're on a bad trip that's just the way it is
you were sixteen you were at a party
the kids with the good grades sipping their drinks
and you smoked some dope and couldn't
think clearly anymore that's the devil man
persecution anxiety religious ideation
and dopamine and serotonin were a door
that opened upon your fractured perception
weed is two things everything is two things
diabolus and these mean assholes in heaven
and you heard your Bach so sad and disturbing
it's not the devil man your buddy says

I said I'm in love I smoked some dope
and Dad's gonna kill me
Dad's so angry Dad has a demon
or Dad drank too much whiskey in Vietnam
I hurt my head too many times I'm in hell
doctor I lied you don't love me it's language

RICH PRODUCER

Oh God, I'm so grateful
I don't have to be a philosopher.

But I do know we return to the Lord
and there's a bit of the Goddess
in each of us.

All I have to do after thirty years
is jot down the little discrete
truths that can't be estranged.
And yes, I take it all with me into
the museum and still
break down everything everybody says.

And I've taken every chance I could.
I'm living here at Parkview Place
thinking about dopamine and the devil
all the while little Marx is right beside me.
Oh, when I was young my dad still said
to put on a crisp white shirt and talk
to the folks at Anheuser-Busch. Yeah, right.
Do I have to be homeless like Morrison?
No, says Red. Morrison made it
because he met the right producer.

GIVEN

I've had the perfect storm of mental illness.
Oh, my enviable brain!
Born breech and several head injuries,
tripping out in South County,
my dad yelling,
completely unmoored in college,

there are so many things I want to tell you
about my early days on West Pine,
sneaking softly into Woolworths
to get a bunch of cheap cookies,
too embarrassed to go into the dining hall,
looking down paranoid as hell from the top
of Pius Library,

prone and freaked out in my bed
after making a fool of myself
in my poetry professor's office
because my buddy always insisted on getting me high
at the most inopportune times.

Now I always have the vague feeling
that I'm some kind of criminal,
clean for nineteen years. I know,
I know, everything has been given to me.

MY HEROES WERE ALL DEAD BY NOW

I've been living under water. No,
that sounds stupid. I've been
living in between things.
That doesn't sound right
either.

But I know I'm a pharmakon
and I don't have a place.
I learned that from reading Derrida,
I believe. And I believe in hell.
And I believe in being unconscious
and that the unconscious
can destroy you.

When I was starting out
I thought a poet
was someone in a lonely room
with wind whipping through the windows
and a bottle and a typewriter on a desk
and some old dying flowers nearby.
I thought a poet
was someone going up against the world,
neither in the world,
and neither of the world.

LETTING GO IN CARBONDALE

Maybe I don't deserve
the wonderful gifts
I've been given.

Oh, I can hear you,
I can hear you loud and clear.

And then the rain begins,
the wind blows through,
a beautiful cardinal alights
in the gutter.

To think that once I was
so arrogant as to think
that any of that
had anything to do
with me.

WORKS ARE DEAD

I have this callus on my knee
from repeatedly getting down
and praying and repenting.
But I think it's thanks
to St paul that today I learned
a new gesture.

So much crazy shit
went down at coffee where I was
corrupted and said like
twelve offensive things.

It was on accident, I maintain!
But still I had to suffer
and come home and feel terrible.
Then, standing by the trashcan
with my soda and cig listening
to Beethoven, I waved
my right arm like a wand over
the vision of Starbucks and pictured
me covering the scene with mad purple
Pollack scrawls and disordered paint
and let it go. So you see that works
are dead.

NULLIFIED

I insist upon divine intervention
and the eucharist
and getting messages
from elevators and stoplights
and the synchronicities
of electric alarm clocks.
As my new analyst has said,
"Electricity is so meaningful to you."

But God has erased everything else I've done
but sitting for a while
with Mr. Bornstein on his deathbed
and lifting twelve stones
for Beatnik Bob's big project
and giving one sixth of my sandwich
to the heroin addict.

I owe a debt of gratitude to so many people
but then that gets nullified
when I imagine they want me dead.
That's all okay. You can still see me
walking with impunity to Starbucks on my
little Romantic Quest. That's where we
commune.

HAPPENSTANCE ON DALE AVE.

I don't ask for very much, just to go back
to the time I sat cross-legged on my bed
and stared so hard at the hippie version
of the Miriam-Webster I'd lifted off my big sister
and its bright yellow tie dye and green paisley
and blue words like "Bummer" and
"Super" and "Ego Trip" and "Right On"
right there on the cover as Dad was in the kitchen
making his angry chili with an inane game on
and Mom was sad on the couch
and no matter what I encountered that night
it would be Emily, Emily forever
who literally and ironically lived on Highland
and this was before so many compromises were made
and the blinds got so dirty we couldn't look
and our old vocabulary got ruined
and next came the never-opened self-help books
or the odd treatise on Romans that gathered dust
and effluvia because sometimes I wish
I'd never said anything at all, never opened my mouth,
just lay down in my very best suit
with my hands crossed on my chest as my eyes were
closed and let whatever was going to happen, happen.

CONTRARY

> *No one will remember*
> *the years they felt nothing*
> 　　　　—Nick Flynn

I'm going to remember
all the years I felt nothing
because I
write about that shit every day.
Oh, I won't stop complaining.
It's going to be my downfall,
this intense anhedonia
and the refusal
to dress it up in a way
that skirts around it
and offers up some common trope.
If you'd like a trope then
there's this:
I got coffee and ink
all over my sheets.

JUST A KID FROM MISSOURI

Telling me that
I didn't have to go nuts
in order to write verse
is like saying
the Beatles didn't have to do acid
in order
to make Sgt. Pepper.

When I ran away
from home
I ended up all the way up
in Alaska, amidst
all the purple sunset volcanoes
and the crazy tide rips.
My captain told me,
"I sailed the Mississippi once,
foot and a half seas and shit . . ."

PROBLEMS

My sister reinjured her horrible knee
and I'm down
here again in Carbondale
to do whatever I can.
Suddenly, last night,
she developed a toothache too
and the cheap doctor can't see her for days
and nothing seems to help.

I tried hiding from God
at the same moment He opened my mouth.
I know that "He" is problematic.
I only say it because
He's the one
who beats the shit out of you.

GRACIOUS

The primary process
was in full effect
when I awoke on the other side
of my door,
confused and with no key

or wallet or shoes
or teeth or tobacco.

After sleeping on a little couch
in the basement
I arose and saw Red
by the elevator. I asked him
what time it was
and it turned
out it was time to go
to Starbucks.

I walked in the rain in
my socks blurry
without my glasses and was given
coffee and cigarettes and a sweater.

Now, if we're wondering
what a Transcendental Signified
is I'm pretty sure
it has something to do
with all of this.

ANOTHER LIFE

I should have stayed in the country
and married Michele and then
none of this would have happened.
I should have just finished my degree
and got a job and started a family
and continued to write songs that rhymed
and then drunker and drunker
smash my guitar on our patio
next to the barbecue pit
and refuse to show up to work
and accuse my kids of being robots
and scream that Michele was CIA
and take down and sully the American flag
and go to several dozen bars
and hook up with students
and lose the ability to speak or write
and come home in rags and throw up
everyone crying and swearing
as Michele calls the pastor
and that doesn't work and I get committed
to an asylum and try to hide out
and end up in a little forlorn room
with my notebooks and a TV and try
to get my shit together. Yes,
that's exactly what I should have done.

A GOOD FIT

I remember stepping so lightly
at midnight out of my room
when I was seventeen
and grabbing the beige phone
from the wall in the kitchen
and there was no dial tone
but a voice there said,
"You'll be hearing from us shortly."

And the next day I left class
with my hips asway
and went out to my beat-up car
and pounded down a bottle of wine
and there were no more
boundaries
and I'd be a heartbeat from homeless
cooled down and autocorrected
and taken over by a call
that launched a thousand pills
and unfortunate psych wards

and last night I dreamt
I was being interviewed on NPR
and they had the audacity
to challenge my
line breaks and I said Hey I
merely tender the words I'm given
and then they brought in ten
crowns and I had to keep
trying them on
until I found the one that fit.

REFRESH

Poetry is sitting
in front of a computer all day
and clicking hearts.

Poetry is a bunch of other poets
know who you are.

Poetry has to do with
hearts.

Poetry is not walking to the post office
a mile away in the blistering cold
with your sad manuscript.

Poetry is noticing stuff
in your neighborhood
that makes little sense.

Poetry is worrying
about accumulating a lot of likes.

Poetry has always been about worrying.

Poetry is you friended
your old high school teacher
whom you told years ago
in tremulous and halting words
you wanted to major in English and Philosophy
and when asked "What will you do with that"
you really couldn't answer,
you were tripped
up.

Poetry is pining for the old mall
where everyone and everything
was beautiful
and you were young.

Poetry is pining.

Poetry is everyone passing
very slowly as you
stand by the bedside perplexed.
Poetry is dumb Zoom
and you telling yourself
at least I don't have to shower.

Poetry is walking back and forth
in the kitchen drinking tons of coffee
and talking to yourself
and brewing up a big explosion.

Poetry is a primary process event.

Poetry is standing atop a mountain
and shouting a bunch of stuff
that only some people get.

Poetry is all mixed up and ambivalent
and putting your arms about the earth
and weeping when your classmate
gets into *The New Yorker* and then
bitter walking around rich Ladue
wondering who won the Pulitzer
in 1988 or '89 or '90.

Poetry is you could reach
the kingdom of heaven if only
you weren't
on the hook for eight hundred dollars
for some diabetes education classes
Medicaid wouldn't cover.

Poetry is going to sleep
and waking up
with blinding lights in front of you
and realizing
you're driving your sister's car
and you're about to hit someone head on.

Poetry is your nurse practitioner
saying everything that's happening
is because you're angry at your dad
so God gives you special dispensation
to write about him
but you're still nervous and timid
as if he's hovering like a superego from hell
with a horrible bite.

Poetry is you were bitten
but you can't remember when or how.

 Poetry is breaking the law.

Poetry is staring at a screen so long
you finally give up and go out
to have a cigarette.

Poetry is everyone's evasive and
your security guard buddy shows your
book to a colleague who wants to meet you.

Poetry is everybody doing their bit
and passing down a little gnosis
and riding the Metrolink with your
MFA pals and reaching out
to touch the metal pole to make sure
that it exists.

Poetry is an explosion in your brain
that says a god came in
and the cosmos will never die
and the Internet
was actually built for you
so you never have to dress up
and go to a reading again.

MY CHARM

I went all the way to grad school
from the boarding home
and I brought my restless black teeth
and my army bag full of relentless scrawls.
While I was ready to attest to what was real
when we were at the picnic
my teacher shouted,
"There's no need to impress anybody here!"
And we're pals now.

But across the street from the boarding home
was a fake library
in which an off-duty cop lingered
and if you went in
screaming bloody murder
after dyeing your hair with coffee in the rain
she would not look at you at all,
wouldn't even flinch. And you
and your new buddies were starting a rock band.

Forget the mirror. It's so easy to tell
when someone's touched. I found an old rolled-
up bag of Top that looked like a yellow bugle
and tried to smoke it. Pretty impressive.

HOT EGGS

I was the only one
at the Carondolet Residential Care Facility
who had any cash
because my sister had given me an hundred bucks
so accordingly
I took Seagraves to breakfast
at a little rinky-dink diner on South Broadway
stopping several times
to roll cigarettes

and as we were waiting on our eggs
I said quite accidentally
a few uncharitable phrases
about Sarah McLachlan
because this was the period
during which I was trying to exorcise her
from my consciousness
and my delusional framework

and then suddenly
some guy in the back barely muttered
"He just killed his sister."
So that Tobasco was invented by the devil.

A PLEA

Something terribly wrong has happened.
I think I've become pure.

Oh God, now I'm going to have to
counsel people and shit. I'm going
to have to relinquish all my possessions.
The Lightning Hopkins CD! And the Mahler!
I'm going to have to leave behind
the dusty old flag in the corner
they gave me at my father's grave.
Now I'm going to have to view the Beatles
as a foolish teenage phenomenon. Well,
I already don't have a car so that's cool.
Shit! Am I going to write platitudes?

I swear I didn't do this on my own.
I was always looking at beautiful people
over coffee at Starbucks. My ridiculous claim
was that it was more about aesthetics than lust.
So I guess I've been proven correct.

And now God has done what I myself refused
to do. Nothing can stir me.
I should have seen this coming
when I kept referring to sex as
an inordinate waste of time. But still,
I was somewhat interested. Now I'm dead.
Now I'm really really dead. I wanted
to be famous but now I'm going to be famous
for having been ripped apart in a Bacchanal.
This is awful. Imagine the weight on my back!
I'm going to be just like Supergirl, no, Wonder Woman.
All my third-grade daydreams are happening.

There are going to be drunks coming
out of the woodwork for advice. People are going
to want to know what to do at work.
It won't matter whether I'm tripping out or not.
I'm on the clock! But what about my own
drunken escapades and horrible utterings
from decades ago? I'm not worthy to say a damn thing.
Please let me loose. I'm weak. Send me elsewhere.

TOOTHPASTE

Bruckner came by the other day
to try and get me to go to a bar
and when I refused
he started talking about the old days.
"Don't you wanna go back
to when we were driving around the
Lindbergh 8 and you shouted to everyone
in line for the movie that you were hot
and they only wished they could have you
but none of them were good enough for you?
Don't you wanna go back to that?"

Oh, my dear Bruckner, I see
you haven't yet been stricken down by
God. And I was hypomanic at nineteen!
It would be like putting
the toothpaste back into the tube.

I know this is sublimation,
I know this is severe repression,
but out of all the dying confusion
and wretched defeat I've cried out
my very own beatitude. I pray you dig it.

WHO I AM

I'm writing little missives to the devil,
trying to conjure him into reality.

You see, all along I thought it was me.

"You can't be crazy if
you think you are," said Lesbia.
But she was the type who could trip and be cool.
I tried stealing a book from the Pius stacks
and when the bell went off I was back
to being a little bird. God's light
gets through to everything.

Don't you love it when a phrase enters
your pulsing brain because now you're
damaged goods, you're smitten, now
you know your dear friend
is hanging out with you ironically.

I just wanted to sing Difference, edge out
the spell. Poor dad with a space heater
in a room too big for it to work.
Shouting matches during dinner. I'm going
back to the beginning, now I know who I am.

RONDO

I'm finally out of time
and I've broken the pattern, now
everything seems like it's moving
so much faster than it really is.

My father banged on a door
and then I banged on a door, but after
a while I stopped banging.
Or the door opened. I'm not sure.

I do know
that I'm just in time,
and that none of this
will be translated.

THE VICTOR

"Hey, Dr Valentine. I want
my discharge papers drawn up
and I want two weeks of meds and I
don't wanna hear any shit. Get on it!"

I've heard it said a popular poet said
sometimes he feels he's on an ambulance
on the way to the psych ward and he's
listening to someone confess their demons.
I won't tell you who quoted that—

Just some prominent St Louis poet
at a prominent workshop in which
he refused to workshop my prominent poem.

Oh sure, I was sad. Then I was mad. And
then I was hurt. Afterwards I was confused.
But I sleep soundly now, unconfined and
free from terror. Sometimes when I'm alone
amidst a big crowd and someone winks
I get a little glance of madness and I
wink back quite confidently. It ain't
just anyone who could put horror in its place.

MY BRIEFEST BRIEF

Dear Dr Valentine, I'm so sorry,
I'm so sorrowful and sad, I know
you thought I'd be cured by now.
But I haven't done anything wrong.
I take my meds, I take part loosely in society.
It's been decades
since I drank or smoked some dope.

Wait a second. I think the Ativan's kicking in.

HEARING BACK

I went from wandering the streets
to wandering the halls
of academe again, haunting
Humphries with a Diet Coke, thinking

"I'm in school right now."
And we were just like early Christians,
commandeering Café Ventana as
my close buddy Matt was like,
I wonder what heresy I'm hearing right now.

So, you're telling me this is the Repeat in History,
a weird trip through the underworld,
and none of the signs were real
and my buddy crying at the bar
was an operation on two levels.

I guess I had to go through things twice.
I had to touch things to know they were there.
I called Lesbia after twenty years
and she called me a psycho. I even
wrote a long pleading letter to no avail
apologizing to the dean of arts and sciences
at NYU. I haven't heard back.

A DEMON!

I have the luxury of not having
to know anything,
and the blessing of not having
to have anything.

I'll tell you something else:
Another miracle took place.
Only my sisters are going to get this.

As I was riding on the 97
on the way to see my nurse
we passed the mental hospital which used
to house me on and off for several years
and I didn't get down and out
with that feeling you simply have to endure,
no, I felt pretty good. Good to be out, sure,
but good for having been there too.

Another kind of lightning struck
when I was zoning out and woke
to hear my nurse saying something about
mania. So that when I left
I went straight down and couldn't stop it
as some demon tried but gracefully failed
to steal my election.

FOR KAYE

I was anointed in an old two-family flat
off South Kingshighway
by a seer who was the boyfriend
of the mother of a young woman
who'd taken me home from LaRocca's
the night before not too long
after I'd gotten out of MPC on Delmar
and I didn't have anything going on except
this silly habit
of scribbling on paper with a cheap pen.

"Now don't start thinking
you're different than anybody else,"
said the seer as hot oil ran down my neck.
He had a wispy goatee and a tattered Cardinal's shirt.
"You've got to relate."

And I've been relating ever since, a useful idiot
in Hardee's and Harpo's, pounding Diet Cokes
at the Hideaway, making zero menacing gestures,
offering up pedantic anecdotes and trying
to make a good sentence, then thinking
about "Sentence," and by the way, Kaye,
I told you that one day I'd write about this.

A BIT OF ALCHEMY

I've had the transgressive impulse, the one
so eloquently described by
my beautiful Romantics scholar at
Saint Louis University.
Every time I clean my dentures
I'm tempted
to throw them hard against
the kitchen floor, smashing them to bits.

It would mean the destruction
of my false self.

On the other hand, when I was at St Mary's
for a minor heart procedure,
the nurse asked me why
someone so young had dentures.
"Let's just say the Freemans
are keeping dentistry alive and kicking,"
was my reply.

A LAMB

I'm operating under the soul here,
even as I don't exactly
even know what the soul is.
Maybe it's what puts the extra unknown
stuff into your verse against your will.
Maybe it's that thing that abolishes
and makes a joke of my forty-seven years.
I'm not grown up at all,
and I've fallen,
and I can't remember
what it was like before I fell.

But my good buddy Anthony gave me a bit
of verse at coffee when I told him
three friends here died and my young drunken
buddy exclaimed that we were in a death trap.
"Death walks the building and no one knows
on whose door it's going to knock."
Not too bad. Almost biblical. I must admit
that as I write this I'm fearful of a jinx.
Words alone have their power. As I left
Starbucks I said maybe I'll kill a lamb
and paint its blood on my door. "I don't think
that kind of thing works anymore," Anthony said.

BOBBY

I met with a shaman
in a room above the old modeling agency
that repped Diana
and I was supposed to find
my spirit animal and I
really really wanted it to be a wolf
but when I got the vision
it turned out to be a rabbit
and of course I was sad and disappointed
but then I thought well a rabbit's productive
and I'd taken a personality test
long ago stoned at Chief's not far away
and Chief's results and the results
of all our friends were that
they all had centered brains
but my area of activity was wildly to the side
but the key thing I remember is
that it said whenever I find out
what I'm here to do I'm going to be really productive
and don't I write poems everyday
and now years later I recall
and old significant family history my dad always told
that my aunt had a pet rabbit
when they were all growing up
and one night my grandpa told my dad
to go fetch a rabbit for dinner and then later
at the table my aunt said this is good
what is this and my dad said, "Bobby."

COUNTER SUBLIME?

I apologize again.
There were so many
beautiful people
who wanted to tear my clothes off.
Couldn't they see that I was all fucked up?
That it wasn't my fault?
That I was frozen inside?

I guess these poems are Christian poems
because they prize doing one thing
while real reality
demands you do something else.
Or maybe I'm just a total loser.

A LITTLE INNOCENT

I've always been into
things you can't touch
and things you can't see

and no matter
how many meds they
make me take
my condition roughly remains the same
because, I've sadly come to know,
the problem's not with my brain,
it's with my soul.

Maybe this is the big one,
the one where I explain everything
and leave vision behind
for good.

But I see the same folks every day
and sometimes they look a little different.
Sometimes a god speaks through them
and they're not even aware of it.
When I said this to Dr Valentine I noted
a slight movement of her upper lip—
indicating disgust.
I couldn't bridge that gap. Game: gone.

SO THAT MAYBE I'M STILL IN THE GAME

I don't feel so bad
about being on SSI
when I think of how the poets
were hooked up in antiquity.
Plus, says my sociologist buddy,
think of all the bad shit
throughout history
that government's done to your ancestors.

Sometimes I almost feel normal.
I start making plans.
Maybe I'll live in a cheap hotel
and play my guitar and harmonica.
Maybe I'll hitchhike to New York
and get discovered on the subway.
Though—I'm already widely known
down under.

But Dr Valentine wants me off Ativan.
I've had persecution anxiety for thirty years!
This is obviously no poetics. I know
all the tricks by now. And it ain't malingering.
Down at Pius, coming out of the medical stacks,
I feel like I've just been hit by lightning.
What do I see but a pair of brown eyes.

IT'S WEIRD THE WAY THINGS TURN OUT

I'm seeing Dr Valentine again.
It's a huge breakthrough.
And I did everything on my own,
nothing was prescribed.
Nothing was proscribed either.

Before our appointment she somehow got wind
that it was the big day
of my first post-pandemic gig
and that I was hoping to meet someone
so she was elegantly made up
and her eyes were bright

and you see I'm in touch with a very
different kind of magic now, one that I have
no control over and one that keeps me
in the dark while my higher power
does all the work.

Speaking of such things has made me aware
that Red and Diana finally hooking up
behind Parkview Place where I smoke means
everything's completed or drastically ruined.
Time will tell. But let's go with completed.

GRANTED

Sometimes I fall into being
just a typical
schizophrenic. After I dreamt
about my dad
a white feather materialized
in the middle of my room. Like
the one John promised to Yoko after death.
And when I couldn't make up my mind
on whether I should sing or read poems
down at the Way Out Club
my guitar strap broke. Someone tried
to hack me evilly and my internet
shut down for reasons apparent
to the AT&T guy but in
my mind it was the work of a demon.

Pronoia! We'll turn that frown upside down.
My nurse mentioned mania and I fought
so hard that when I left her office
I was escorted by angels. And then
the venlafaxine levelled off and I noted
happily the disintegration of the negative symptoms.
You can't make this magnetic shit up. My idea was
I was afraid of death and then was granted life.

DAMNING

The first displacement
from science
into the difference of the symbolic
took place in the fourth grade
when I decoded
and copied down the entry
in the encyclopedia for "Lightning"
into my little red notebook.
And I loved Ms. Ehret.

I'm part of this world
but I'm not a part of that world
and that makes a big difference.
You think
you can sit down at the bar
and have a conversation
with a buddy you played ball with.
Not true. You're going
to make a great motion
sitting there on the stool
among the damning and stultifying
undercurrents
as the bartender comes back
from break
with a tiny bit of white powder
on her upper lip.

TIRED

I asked my nurse if she thought
it was possible my problem
was not with my brain
but with my soul. Well, she said,
everything's connected.

They say nothing's got for nothing
but everything I have
was given to me for free.
And if no one had ever mentioned the soul
I doubt that I would have dreamed it up.
I am being compensated, however,
for my war against time.

Today I'm sick to my stomach
as I think about dear Mozart.
I think someone at the pharmacy
scribbled all over my bottle of Ativan
but I'm too tired and disgusted
to make my usual
paranoid interpretation.

THANKS

It's thanks
to a chronic illness
that I can function so well.

Oh, you should have seen me
back in the day running
around the ward
one minute trying to escape
and the next telling my doctor
I'd found the cure for schizophrenia.

"I even wrote a book about it,"
I claimed, "and the whole time I had
'You're The One For Me, Fatty' on repeat."
"Morrissey, you know,"
I indicated to the young doctor sitting in.

Now I've somehow achieved
boulevard status in the biggest of ways
and as I check myself out in the mirror
while I'm getting ready for the family reunion
way out in the suburbs
I know I still have the embers
of something that set me on my way
and I know
it's got to do with language.

DISSIPATION

I've returned at last! And
I'm pondering
all those sweet high school things
like knowledge causes pain
and all the major themes and conflicts
and the denoument and the soul
and a part of me is a part of the world
and Spleen and the Ideal

and math and painting and poetry
are all really the same thing
and it's the soul in you
that performs the big aesthetics

and I'm walking around everywhere
with no regard for time
and I'm still thinking about electricity
and our old house on Dale that
burned down and I'm smiling
at all the different people I pass
and for a moment
I might feel shame and horror when
I know I'll never go back to Scholars House
but all that dissipates quickly
as I pass the cracked
stone circle
where all the stoners sit
a pass along the swift and stiff
symbolic phenomenon.

SMALL

Fearless is
when you write faithfully
about psychosis
and misinterpreting signs again
and ending up in the hospital because
you asked again for
the paramedics to take you
to your doctor because you accidentally
took a month of meds in ten days.

And you meet someone cute
at Blueberry Hill and when they
ask what you do you follow the advice
of your sister and your grad school friends
and say, "I'm a writer" and not "I'm a poet"
but as the conversation proceeds
you know
it's just a matter of time
before they figure out somehow
that you are recovering still from schizophrenia.

Well, I don't live in linear time
and every time I go back it hurts and it's
embarrassing and the fact
that all this was written ages ago
is only a small comfort.

IT WASN'T ME

A fierce prophet with wild hair
and some mood disorder or worse
who fixates on Time
in his lonely little room
and will probably never have babies
and whose gender is neither relevant nor
definite and who isn't afraid
to damn the evil pestilence
and who got called and saw the light
and clumsily opened his mouth
when the birds suddenly came into Being
and who sits at a computer for three hours a day
and learned to mix metaphors in his mom's
basement when God or a god was there
and the doors opened and a breeze came in
and The Other became such a lovely puzzle
and who sits
at a Platonic Coffee wondering
in dismay having fallen so hard
how it was to get back up
and climb into this beautiful dream.

IT ENDS WITH THE DEVIL

Ladylove asked me when my voice
was going to change. Like,
what I might sound like ten years from now.
Because I keep saying the same thing over and over.
I thought about it, and my guess
was was
that it was going to take a big change of consciousness.
I think tonight it happened.
Before I read poems at the marimba concert at Joe's Cafe
I caught the eye of one of the musicians
and she came over and we had the most beautiful conversation
and I couldn't believe it as I gazed upon her bare shoulders
I could not believe that this was actually happening
and I knew I had to forget everything high school Bruckner had told me
and then I went out back and it was crazy
there was a huge old heavy anchor
and there was a rusty Gaelic cross and wild light bulbs
and there were 1950's robots and there were random
synchronous street signs with meaning and there
was a sign that actually said half god because we die
and before I even had a chance to sort this through
a sense of peace came over me and I admit I'd taken
extra Ativan and I realized how heavy it had been
to walk around feeling always that everyone hated me and my reading
was beautiful and I made some cash I dearly needed and I waved forlorn
to the wonderful musician when we left and Beatnik Bob
mentioned in passing she's in Rolla tomorrow
and I came home and put on my earbuds and had a smoke
and a Diet Dr Pepper while listening to some good music
but then Red came up and I could barely hear him but oddly
he was talking about the price of bus tickets to Rolla. I think.

I APPROPRIATE THE LITERAL

I was outside smoking behind
Parkview Place with my iPod and Diet Dr Pepper
making a vain attempt at relaxing when
my young homeless destitute writer buddy
came up to the fence again to bum a cigarette
so I turned off the music
and got up at length
and brought my pouch and papers to the fence
and tried not to touch his fingers
during the major COVID transaction
and he's been so quiet and in a trance
I even earlier at first thought he was a ghost
and I'm such a dolt I took it literally
when he said he was looking for his family
because now I can apply the several
severe interpretations
that have a lot to do with hippies and vampires
or really anyone with really big eyes
like a social worker who paints on the side
but I tell you I have a good heart
and remember all too well what it was like
turned loose into the boarding home
where the literal and the symbolic merged into one
so he's talking about someone
who will take him in and teach him
how to reconstruct the ego because now he's living
in the unconscious
and it's clear he's given everything he's got
and ought to be some spectacular genius or rock star
and what exactly separates us
because why do I have a domicile and struggle

for peace and put on Enya and write
and say things straight out with no patience for any criticism
and once too was radiated by the universe
and heard the same call walking away
and able to hear whispers from a hundred yards behind me
without one dull scholar who could understand it and I am thinking it's not enough
to say we're on different sides of the fence as he rises up and puts his arms
in the air and walks over to the circle where the stoners sit like an errant god
and damn I haven't made that move since the observation room in 2001.

AN INCOMPLETE CONCLUSION TO THE EVIL PESTILENCE

Well, I'm not paranoid today.
I may be bummed out, but I'm not paranoid.
And maybe my sister is right,
maybe my poems aren't offensive.
You know, my old MFA pals
said it's okay to mention women.
They even said you could say they're pretty!
Wow, I'm belated now, all that seems so absurd.

I'm always mentioning
my many possessions
and my dear fabulous expulsion
and how I called my mom from Columbia
at Mid-Mo in the middle
of Missouri and begged her to come sign me out
but so presently I fear
that if I had stayed there for a while now
I'd be rich and famous. Somehow
I really messed up.

JUST FOLLOWING

I don't feel like my time is my own—
maybe that's why intuitive Adam the Jewler
said I could do whatever I want.
His name is Lieberman,
so I guess we're brothers
in irony.

I think I gave birth in prison!

Oh, there are such dejected and forlorn
phrases running around my head
that must confuse
most of my friends who find me
so cheerful. Once a med student
in the research program said, Matt,
you'd have to be really down, I'm saying
really very down for anyone to notice.
I'm just sitting here and spitting out what arrives.

So now my hope's invested in the fact
that I heard that Vanilla Ice likes poetry.
I've got to get my books to him! One more time
for Gen X, Vanilla and Freeman together,
the whole new album would just write itself.

I DARE SAY

It might not exactly have been manna,
but I did come across
a package of beef stew and a can of pork and beans
on the bench by the elevator.

I'm learning to fly again. Things aren't the same.
I don't think I'm a real human being with feelings.

We're going to experience the forthcoming
small tragedies having been left behind
by a God we only think is quiet
and the big long reaching arm of kapital.
I'm faithful to the famous Slovenian sage.

My Diet Dr Pepper is going to run out
and my iPod fall fallow,
then they're going to outlaw all cigarettes.

And I'm going to blame the craven poststructuralists.
I fought them in vain for eighteen years.
The dull folks who were in the same classes
would say So love someone.
I would say repent.

SPENT

When you awake and realize
that you're in an allegory—
well, nothing is better.
You see,
you've known this was coming
since you were a kid.
But you could never name it.
It's why you slept on the floor all night
outside Lesbia's door—but when
she finally took you in
you couldn't quite open your mouth.
You're going to spend—and be spent—
the rest of your life trying
to name it, pissing
away a scholarship and rising up
only to go off the rails.
Some people call it schizophrenia.
Some people say you've ingested a god.

Last night my sister said that her aged
lonesome friend upon her final bed said
repeatedly she wished
she could fly from her body like a bird.
Sometimes I don't feel like a poet. Sometimes
I just feel like an asshole putting words together.

MEASURED

By any sane stable measure
in the heavily belated
late liberal free neo-conservative
market,
I'm an abject failure.

People malign Little Marx
but without him and the mixed economy
I'd be dead meat. On a side note
I would mention
that I might already be dead meat
because I think
my blood stopped flowing. But
that's for a different poem.

Maybe they should make social programs for
poets. Rotten teeth? Check. Afraid of sex? Check.
But without some capital there'd be no marginal
friction. And regardless of
whatever psych evals they give
they still don't know where
poetry comes from. You can be a loud asshole
and write quiet poems. You can be
silent for years
and then come out with some
bombastic revelations. I thank my good buddy
Chief, who remarked when I said I was a loser,
"Artists are held to a different standard."

IPOD, DIET DR PEPPER, CIGARETTE

There's a philosophy somewhere
that posits
that almost everything
is a bunch of bullshit
and will fade away and be forgotten.
My father was a strict unconscious
adherent to this.

And I was too! But when I knew
what I needed to do
every phenomenon I came across
fell into service
of that one little thing.
Maybe that's why
I gave to my shadow the permission
to screw everything up so wildly
at SLU and NYU.

But now when I sit behind Parkview Place
right in the midst of my life
with all the accoutrements I need
and I see the kids off to class
with their skateboards and scooters
I get a wonderful vibe
without any bitterness or regret
and I wish a blessing
for their most deep and fervent dreams.
I have no real explanation for this.
You just wake up
and twenty years have gone by and you're
different. "You need to think
about revisions," my sister says.
And Diana says, "I can talk now when I'm stoned."

NO DOUBT

I wrote a song and I'm kind of elated—
I thought I'd never write a song again.
But, believe me, no one wants any lyrics.
Everyone knows that the consciousness
that goes into a poem could probably power
a hundred songs. You'd just need a lot of coffee.

So now I'm in a different vibe, I'm locked into a vision—
I'm seeing all our old haunts in Dogtown,
with all the old dudes singing
and a guy at the end of the bar with his head on the bar
while no on really cares. That's how it used to be!

Words are just coming in and asking for chords.
No one's going to listen, and anyway Ladylove tells me I'm
a cheap Dylan ripoff. But I don't even give a shit!
I'm not drinking,I haven't taken any drugs,
and I've got to use this time
because at all other times I'm proccupied with spleen.
I just have to figure out what God wants from me.
Therefore I'm going to walk
down to Forest park and go into
that secret spot by the art museum
where years ago I hid my corduroy coat
so no one would recognize me. I'm calm,
I'm ready, I'm all prepared for the next
new interpretation and the necessary
Repeat in History to set me free.
But I've got to hurry and get organized
because I can already hear doubt creeping in.

INTO HIMSELF

I put one fourth of an oven pizza
in front of my dad
and he said,
"We sure eat pretty good, don't we."
A rigor was soon to set in.

And at that time I never thought
how getting this down might be holy.
I just thought I was playing
with words.

STANDS FOR SOMETHING ELSE

Whenever I go back to New York
there I am finding myself
again at Shades of Green
comforted in knowing so much time has passed
and telling my buddies to belly up to the bar
and chanting out the borderline bardic
statements. My life has become
an apology.

I am a dedicated follower of Big Pharma
and diet soda. My memory
is all messed up and I'm a machine.
When I walk now to Forest Park
with my one and only desire
I fret over my thoughts and feelings
and hope to insert them into the Mind of God
before everything's ripped apart
and burned alive
and it's funny how a pill can deliver you from hell
and into the upper regions of purgatory

but let me just write down exactly what happens
so you can say
Oh! What an excellent allegory!

TECHNOLOGY FREAKOUT

Oh Starla, my God, when I thought
you had blocked me on Facebook
I immediately
went into this completely terrific hell
with the demon of every misstatement
I'd ever made come up to mangle me
and walking to get a slinger at the Peacock Diner
was the most difficult thing I'd ever done
as I went through a crucible of the consciousness
and tried to turn around the accusations
into the perspective that really I'm just stupid and innocent
and with great effort
also attempted a variety of interpretations

and I think we're cool now and it was just a mistake
and I'm all emptied out
and Oh I promise to keep my mouth shut from now on
except to say that you're wonderful and I'm so sorry
and I am a calm disinterested outcast just like St Paul

and I'm trying to conceive of just one thing again,
one idea in the sun,
maybe even something sublime,
like that old feeling you got
when they let you out of jail one morning
after having been banned from the Cheshire Inn
and a complete change of person is called for.

WHAT'S TO LOVE

I walk a little quieter when
little Enoch is around.
I have said that he is holy.
I know that you, dear reader,
would probably think
that he's clearly suffering
from some unknown
malady.

I can't tell you what we do here all day
but there is a structure to it.
There's a rhythm. You can call me the drummer.

Today I discovered a secret method
for rising out of hell. But don't tell anyone!
It's five hundred milligrams of Clozaril.
I think though I'm not sure that I'm the only one in the know.
Walking in the rain's different from looking out the window.

I arrive later at Tower Grove Park
with my notes
and continue to put down the penetrating paranoid vibe
and so I can take part
in the psychotic discourse but
what's much more interesting to me
is figuring out those tulips and what's to love.

TAXED

And I've seen that it's possible
to never come out of hell
and that any revisions that are made
are made in the rain.

I knew a guy at MPC on Delmar
twenty years ago now who with trembling fingers
would chain smoke
discarded cigarette butts he found
and whatever was going on in the sky
was contending in his own mind.
He was closer than I can explain.

Other patients would talk about him
and various rumors and reasons
for his condition were passed around.
I felt that they all fell flat.

I don't know what could explain
the sheer dignity and unutterable grace
of someone so painfully and somehow
beautifully cast about.

There's somebody somewhere
paying for every little thing that we do.

GRANDMA RUTH PLANTING FLOWERS

Having felt frozen inside
for the better part of twenty-four years
I find
that at least I can talk and talk,
tell my cousin at lunch at Three Kings
I'm blowing up on Twitter,
I can say things that are relatively appropriate
and don't really take anything anywhere

because my instinct's been flushed down some
galactic black hole and come out
the other side into a multiverse
that whispers to me only when I dream
of having a whole lot of dates and thick hair
and I'm wearing the hip new kind of leather jacket

so you can say that some of us
are just the innocent victims driven mad
by the strictures of capital
and yelling fathers that still yell from beyond the grave
or you can say that we're a bunch of deadbeats
look at that guy he could sweep a floor

and I'm not calling from middle ground no I'm saying
something wholly Other and Ideal
and courting the Real as I asked our neighbor
Grandma Ruth if her granddaughter Jenny would like to play
and she said "why don't you ask her yourself"
and in that so pregnant moment
eight years old the whole course of my life was determined.

DROP THE MICROPHONE SCENARIO

So the whole project was sickness.
I was just out back rolling a cigarette
and taking some Cherry Zero Sugar Dr Pepper
when it began to rain.
It won't rain forever, I thought,
and then I'll make my escape
clean and awake.
And then they took my next door neighbor
to the hospital with the Delta Variant.
I'd been on the elevator with
her as she was coughing and maskless.
She was coughing up a storm. I pray for her.
If you're reading this
it will become impossible to find me.
And you'll never know what thunder rumbled in my brain.
I have a couple of days left to study
Blake at our convivium.
Poor Livingston has passed and I've been cut loose.
It may rain again
so I better quit the continental philosophy.
I'm going to write songs from now on.
I'm going to be sad, I'm giving up television, stupid sitcoms.
I'm leaving all my notebooks behind
and I'm going to sit in that little diner off Washington Square
where Cherry dumped me and broke my heart into
two.

FORGET WHITMAN

Ah, so it's the moon
that's been influencing me.
All these years and I thought it was the sun.
What a fool I was!
I mistook being terribly uptight for stability.
I thought letters involved restraint.

I've been thinking a lot about myself
and what I've discovered is
that the structure of my negative symptoms,
the wonder wall,
is slowly coming apart.

I had a pleasant talk with an intelligent
and amiable older woman today
and when I came home I felt safe and understood.
Maybe later when I put on the Bach some feeling will come.
Maybe I'll feel like going somewhere.
Maybe when I try to take a nap
I'll actually rest.

I'm becoming devout! My mind's still a little messed up
and I'm still writing poems all day with lots of cuss words
and I'm still cussing out the devil
and I'm down with all the forms of witchery
but Christ is handling my dispossession
and Superman's going to sweep up all my sympotoms
and throw them into the sun and then plant my flag on the moon.
Finally, dear Ladylove, it's happening!
The chage in consciousness we talked about to change my stance.
There's a sign and it doesn't have to be a sign.
It's all about aesthetics and forgiveness.
Forget Whitman, John Keats is going to be my guide!

NOVEL

I'm reading the most recent Jay McInerney
and it's making me so sad
because I miss Manhattan so much
and all of the sublime opportunities I threw to the wind
blind drunk and screaming at people in my paranoia
and I don't know how to fix it or forgive myself
when I think I might have been in the Hamptons
writing most elegant verse
and I recognize that McInerney is a master
but down here South Hampton means something much different
as in getting rudely accosted at Dirt Cheap
by a belligerent meth-head hoosier
for absentmindedly failing to let a woman in line
take your place
and then waiting outside red-faced for the forlorn Hampton bus
and as I read I see dear Corrine sad on the summer house porch
and I can totally relate to that passage because
for much of the day I am freaked out with the phrase
"fucking shit" coursing through my head
and as for splendid conversation here
I was just down on the patio smoking with my buddy Red and he said,
"I heard it's gonna cool down a bit, and then
it's gonna get really cold, and by that time it'll be Winter."

WALLET SO SLIM

Thanks to the beneficent
government
which affords to give me
a modest check for my ailments
I'm allowed to employ my Ideals.

And yet last night I had to wait
at Washington and Tucker for forty-two minutes
on the 97 with a wallet so slim
I couldn't even go in anywhere
and get a Diet Coke.

I am called to suffer!
You can't die young on me, Livingston,
and expect me not to write about it.
Was that you calling out to me
outside my nurse's office
after she took me again through
the Repeat in History?
I'm solid, I just had to beg for mercy.

And it's all been decided above.
I definitely won't need to microdose now
that I've written about the dead
and consequently tripped my ass off.
I've never felt so alive

and I've never written what's so true.
And I refuse to make any revisions.
I'm dealing with a lot of dark shit here
but I'm not afraid because I recognize the feeling
from thirty years ago when I was just an ephebe.
And the truth is that I love everyone
who fucked me up, put a spell on me, laughed when I was in hell.

POPSICLE STICKS

I have been on both sides of The Law.
There's the paradigm that says
"These meds will keep me out of the hospital."
And then there's the paradigm that says
"I want to be a shaman like Jim Morrison
and live on a roof like he did
and do whatever's offered to me."
Only you can decide what works for you!
And no, this ain't imperialism.
You can't fight imperialism from Barnes-Jewish.
In fact, at that point you're under it.

Sometimes I am tempted and don't know what to do.
And maybe each path contains part of the Other.
Still, I have to walk into Wendy's and say,
"I'd like two double cheeseburgers to go."
I don't know what discourse that is.

Oh, everything. And when there's nearly nothing
objective you can say about the unchained phenomena
that keep coming in you revert to langauge.
It's cool to write a sentence on reform and get burn holes in your shirt.
It's hard to function when you're tripping unmoored, radically free,
riding the 97 to the end of the line.

It turns out our whole system
was constructed
with flimsy popsicle sticks!

THE SWEET THEORIST AT SLU

Writing spells death. Obviously.
Not only the dissolution of your memory
but the fragmentation
of your whole personality.
Take a look at this sweet new tombstone.
All along you've wanted to know secrets,
like find a secret structure or something
that would provide an overarching theory.
But listen to the wind whispering to you
and see the stoplight change just when you think, "Free."

Or maybe when I was a little boy
I'd race away from the sandlot
and run into the house and up the stairs
and shake my mom awake
and say,
"Mom, I've got so much to tell you!"

BOMB

I ran into my old case manager.
I think it was because
of this sweet leather jacket that Anthony gave me
to a large extent
that she was so interested in what I was up to.
"Time doesn't exist anymnore," I said.
"You may recall what I hinted about Repetition."
For any of this to be true you would have to admit
that we're about to be swallowed by the Real.
I've been getting anxious and incredible vibe.

So everyone flashes in and out of existence.
They have said what's beautiful stays forever.
My simple and ongoing process is to say
I'm sorry over and over until it sticks.
I don't want to fool around with insanity anymore
or make the mistake of dumbly
walking down Delmar and passing by
all the bright phenomena that might save me.

I've gotten to the point where
I'm behaving in the manner in which
an adult would behave. I've learned
that one must eat breakfast and take one's meds.
I've been working every day for a long time!
And my rich buddies believe in me,
they think I'm the bomb. I don't know how that happened,
maybe it's the Transcendental Signified,
maybe it's Intelligent Design,
but maybe it's the leather jacket.

SENSE

I want to write something
that errupts
into an enormous meaning,
something that shines a light
on a heretofore undiscovered truth,
in fact I want to put my whole life into the page,
so that when I die I will know
that the biggest risk possible paid off,
and that all of the claims I made
when I was young and full of wine
at Scholars House
came correct.

MOUTHING OFF TO MY ANALYST AND THEN APOLOGIZING

Having never had a real job,
embraced by the fullness,
I just endured
a twenty-six minute lecture
on Kung Fu
at Starbucks.

Now the time has come
for me to express myself and call together
all the lonesome disparate parts.
If I say something like "freaked out" or "sane"
you better believe
I've earned the right to do it.
I'm going to take all of my calendars
and my schedules and my 3X5s
and burn them and scatter the ashes.
I'm going to unplug my alarm clock
and throw it against the wall.
These are acts of mercy.

Everything's fluid and flashing
in and out of eternity.
Sure, I whispered something
banal and critical at Starbucks
but I don't think
anyone could hear me.
I'm the meekest of the meek!
And I'm only asking for a reprieve.

STARTING AGAIN

I've come quite a long way
from when Julia took me to lunch
and the cashier thanked her
for feeding a homeless man. Sad.

And yet I still have to witness
an escalating verbal assault
between two homeless buddies outside Starbucks
that nearly becomes physical.
And I become a little boy cowering
as his parents go at it again.

Then Adam the Jeweler comes in
and generously gives me
a big bag of tobacco
and a ton of papers.
And Chief takes me to Mike Duffy's
where the bartender gives me
a very long look.
I swear it's the sweet leather jacket
which Anthony gave me.
It's totally changed my life.
"Tell the bartender that Matt
says hello," I chime
to our waitress.
It's been nineteen years
but the miracles are slowly starting again.

OH, THE COMPLICATIONS PSYCHOSIS CAUSES

It's going to be very tense and amazing
when I have to meet
my favorite famous beloved songwriter
and admit embarrassedly that I've mentioned him
a few times in my poems.
I imagine myself starting,
"You see . . . I used to be kind of sick . . ."
Or maybe, "I'm lots better now but
back in the day I suspected you'd written me a song."
I can't see any way of not creeping him out.

And then maybe my other vision will come true,
walking into Barnes-Jewish
amnd claiming I got famous—oh wherefore
this strange relation to fame—
and every time I walk along Forest Park
amid the beautiful falling leaves
everyone's smirking and talking about me
and now I need a place to hide
and no these aren't delusions.

I have been trying to reach out
and I've been wanting, and I never asked
for such an occlusive introversion
and anyway I wrote most of those old poems
when I was high as hell and manic on Zyprexa.
But when I went today to get
my CBC at St Mary's
I looked at my admission record
and under "Employer" it said "Poet."
So if it's true, if I've been dead for many years,
I can't imagine any of this
is really that important.

FREEMAN STRIKES AGAIN

When I was old at twenty-three,
laboring under the Shock of Recognition,
wrestling against the Impossible Thing
and my own disgrace, having been
expelled from the most liberal school in the land,
embarrassed, astonished, ashamed and sad
that I'd never been a Beatle,
something much louder
than my earlier freaked-out reading
of Celtic mythology
came in and seized me.

I made a complete break of every fetter
and peered out from behind
the letters which once had saved me
and which were becoming wildly new
and I was not convinced
that I was going to make it through
all of this.

But it's the soul that makes the outward things.
Yesterday the pain went away
as I was having my cigarette out back
and suddenly I had so many things to say
and Adam the Jeweler texted and said
he had a lot of tobacco and Tops for me
and I went back up to look at my meager bank account
and found my SSI check had hit early
and then I gazed at the TV
and they were celebrating in Atlanta
the great home run master Hank Aaron and a young player
came up and embraced him and what did it say
on the back of his jersey: Freeman.

SPOTTING IT

I was desperately unclean, in the archaic sense,
stinking and thinking the CIA was after me
when God came in
to burn me up. Now I know
it wasn't punishment, it was purification.
It was the best blessing in the realm of possibility.

Shit, you think a journal dedicated
to consumers or clients or patients
or whatever you want to call us—survivors—
would eat this stuff up.
But maybe not! Maybe I should say
that I've searched and searched for many years
and finally found a doctor I can talk to
and we're working on a new fabulous treatment plan.
Who'd want to hear
about a nifty numinous expulsion
and the dread ability to communicate
throughout a wretched blasted conflagration!

A change in consciousness is a change in order.
You're becoming light, you shine.
When little Enoch comes back
and goes straight to the guard's desk you alone know why.
I could go back. I could submit to oppression and repression
and speak and say, far out, man, and hear
this isn't your job, Matt, and respond
no this is exactly what my job is
and I could open a window and I could walk out a door
and empty myself into a world that's not exactly there—
but know it's so hard to ask for help when
you feel like everyone hates you.
No matter, and as they say, if you spot it you got it.

SOME KIND

Damn, right when I think I'm ready
I recoil and have to face
myself and I forfeit
out of this great angst God
has granted to me.
I could have been triggered by too
real talk at Starbucks.
There's always poverty.
Maybe I could work for an ad agency and get rich!

When I try to pin down the exact moment I died
I get so confused by symbols.
But I'm writing this
while still wearing the sweet leather jacket.
I know I loved so well
and rode my bike up and down
Highland Ct.
in the hopes I might see Emily.
And later drove so far
to Terra Haute
to spend the night with Lesbia.
Years later and I get it.
I think the devil thinks I'm some kind of idiot.

Don't fall anymore, says the big fat critic,
and quit looking for sources.
You're forty-eight years old and everything is brand new.

WHAT?

It's such a sublime privilege
to end up with a diagnosis
of schizophrenia.
But I can't tell you why.
It's a secret.
You might refer to my back pages.

But to have the intuition back in the day
at Scholars House up on the women's floor
sleeping on Lesbia's doorstep
that someday all of these bad trips
would be turned into simple validation—
it was some consolation of a sort.
And I never said the whole
of the medical discourse was rotten.

Time out of mind, I thought
that a complete emptying out was a higher good.
But the repurcussions did come
as when she and I were in Forest Park
and I threw a stone at a murder of crows
and they scattered scared and stiff
into a wood which never could be reached.
Dark days, my friends, and gravid too.
What we really want to do's
becoming more and more impossible.

MY YEAR

Wow, I think I'm finding
that I can almost get myself excited
about things and reach out into the world.
I had to call my aunt and say I was sorry
for all the wildly inaccurate things I said
when I called her from the mental hospital.
Listen: You don't want to go to the other side.
There's nothing there but death and destruction.
I'm forty-eight. It's the year my buddy Kerouac died.

AN EXPLANATION

I have succeeded
in threading
the fucking needle.

My prize was the miraculous
extra wafer
that suddenly appeared
during communion
and my new sweet leather jacket.

There was a daemon lurking
again on the patio last night
and my dear homeless buddy
was quite possibly on something new
when in
an almost plaintive speech
he complained that he had cancer
and his hair was falling out
and he was cold. I have such mad respect
but I could see this coming,
the complete dissolution
of the ego.
Though I didn't think
it would happen this quickly.
I begged him to go to St Mary's.

What I've been trying to do
is explain to you
why my family thinks I have a job
and why walking from Starbucks
with my big book on Blake
a pretty woman thinks I'm a possibility.
Like, I just woke up
but I can't quite remember my dream.

HAVING PAID ATTENTION IN MATH CLASS

Damn, I need to be delivered every day.
It used to always involve a bunch of Ativan
but now a kind word
can almost pull it off, or an ephemeral laurel,
or the memory
of waking up next to Persephone.
I can't say for certain whether or not I wanted
to lose my mind.

When I was taking a dumb walk in the park
my glasses fogged up
so I knelt and prayed
and they quickly became clear.

And then a big score coming home
and getting off the elevator—a package of beef stew!
You see, things are working in my favor.
Maybe the old days are done,
all that needless suffering.
I didn't really enjoy it anyway. What a waste!
Sure, I may have gotten a few good poems out of it,
but really, who gives a shit.

I keep getting closer and closer,
and it has a lot to do with the new sweet leather jacket.
But I have to keep reminding myself
not to say anything stupid when I get elevated.
It's like that thing from long ago in algebra—
you know, where the curving line
is heading for that straight line,
inching ever so near
but never in a million years actually touching it.

THEIR WORLD

When I went to get my blood drawn
down and out at Mid-Mo
after my second break
with what the world says is reality
I lazily lay out my limp arm
and the smiling nurse said,
"You've got to pump it up,"
and all I could do was smirk
at this little bit of inside knowledge.

And now years later at Parkview Place
I am finally filled with sorrow
as I sip my soda and smoke my cigarette
and I think back to manic Bruckner
who in high school
would always exclaim, "Let's get pumped up!"
Because I am soon to get glad,
I see the beautiful people passing by
and I'm getting ready to get back
into their world.

SOME IMPORT TO NAMES

I loved my mom and I loved my dad
and I'm sorry that I went nuts.

It's just that the primary process got unloosed
so you can imagine the things I said
and the phone calls I made
as I felt I was following my intuition.
I thank God every day that social media didn't exist back then.

I've been spared all those horrors of fascism.
And the Hoosier Rebellion was only
some monstrosity I watched on TV.
I was able to turn it off and walk to United Provisions
and get some soda and donuts with my food stamps.

I was raised in the center
of the Missouri Synod and surrounded at once
by the paternal metaphor which eclipsed my dad
and I'm glad in a way that all of that was shattered.
I got to figure out my own totem and taboo.
Those Lutherans would probably think it's silly
the way I learned to cross myself so much.
But it's still fun to read awful Luther ripping on the pope.

I wish my mom and dad could see
that with great difficulty I've put my boundary back up
and have recognized
that they were correct about so many things.
I would remind them that when I first left home
and ended up studying French for a summer at Mizzou
my buddy Chief and I would frequently sneak
into a club called "Shattered."

MORE HERESY

It's so hard
to say something
without really saying it.
That's the mission.

But when a second wafer
suddenly appears in your hand
during communion,
that's reality
and there's no getting around it.

There's a scientist somewhere
working at all hours in the lab
trying to figure out
how to tell his buddy's wife
that she's beautiful
without compromising himself
or pissing everybody off.

I'm becoming a real person again
and so many literal
things are taking shape
that I'm being scooted over into
a new discourse. I haven't
felt this way since Chief and I
were in college,
right before I violently
had to rip the curtain apart
and take a look
at what was going on
behind the altar.

MY DREAMS

I keep waiting
for someone to call me up
and ask me to be a professor
but it just never happens.

When I showed up at the MFA picnic
everybody thought I'd been in another fight
because I was missing a couple more teeth
but the truth was that they'd just rotted away.
And then my fame increased
as I was asked to give an oration
to the assembled young writing kids.
I explained how I'd nearly beaten
schizophrenia after fifteen years on Clozaril.
"The medical discourse says it's all dopamine," I went.
"But the trip I'm on indicates the devil."
An awkward moment came later when a fan
walked in on me when I was trying to roll a cigarette
in the john, having failed
to lock the door. As ever, I quit the scene
only moments before the orgy began.

So I'm normal now. Everywhere I go
people in tatters or three-piece suits
come up close and tell me their story.
They have wild hair and speak with great urgency.
But miraculously, I don't think
their speech has anything to do with me
per se. I hear stuff about pro wrestling,
someone tells me he has a friend who's a bus driver,
someone complains about her ex, who happens to

be a pretty good piano player. I have my own thing
but I don't know what to call it, I talk
to my cardiologist about how I was born
on the ame day as Artaud. I suspect everything
is hinging on a dream I had a long time ago,
I'm getting ready to go back to the Dickman building
for analysis, right by Dunaway books where for a while
my poems were in the window.

BETWEEN ANALYSIS

Look at me dealing with dopamine and the devil.
I'm glad those early chaotic days are over.
You should have seen me
down in Union, Missouri, jumped
by twelve guys after
Bruckner thought it would be hilarious
to tell everyone that I was the one
who threw the beer bottle on the roof at the party.
See how I awake on the cold concrete floor
with LOC in a nearby random garage
as the EMS bus rushed rapidly toward us.
Oh, I should have gone to Hollywood.
But, damn, I can't act. We've proven that!
I walk around the Loop here without any affect at all,
there are just a few simple gestures I make
when I want to give the impression
that I'm really intelligent. I carry my book,
but I hide the title because it's just a trashy thriller.
I really want people
to think I'm reading Sartre or Kierkegaard.

Now that it looks like the Leather Jacket Discourse is coming
to its close and I'm done reaching out
I can say with confidence that I wasn't just another asshole
trying to put his imagination onto the world,
I was just drifting along and for a moment the world came into me,
and now that it's dissolving and I never even got to make a date
I'm comfortably down again and tripping out
and I suppose that's just going to have to be my narrative.
At least until my next analysis appointment.
We'll see what I figure out then.

IS THAT IRONY

I'd come close to breaking
my oh-so-cool professorial-looking glasses
many times but yesterday I finally did it.
They fell off my nose
and when I grabbed them close to my heart
God took them away.
I still have the sweet leather jacket
and I'm trying to restore my game
but it's becoming obvious that something is ending.
I'd gotten involved with depreciating values.
What if, what if, I might just find out how Job felt.
Oh, who cares, everything's dead anyhow.

I'm getting as moody as I was back at SLU
where it seemed I had to go to the emergency room like twice a week,
stupidly mixing things up, as if my dad were on steroids.

But no, no, I saw objective things in the environment
that had deep personal meaning for me.
I wasn't making a trivial objective correlative
and it wasn't the effects of ancient speech on my brain.
To really figure it out would involve a deep understanding
of Time. But when I was up in that old wooden loft
I was tossing and turning at the age of eighteen
while something radically new was entering me
and I could hear the disturbing RA going from door to door
to see who was moving in
and everything was changing, it hurt a little,
I was rigidly set against all transference
and everything I'd pushed down was coming back
and I was about to say something spectacular,
I was about to speak in a variety of manners
of the real pulsing truth which was moving in and
out of being.

FOREVER

So, I had to learn
all the things one has to learn
while losing one's mind

and now I'm learning
the things most people learn
at a much earlier age.

They say whatever's repressed
will always return, but
that's not the resurrection.
The resurrection
is standing sad and cold at the bus stop
one night in disfavor for forty-two minutes
and then the next night
going to an elegant party
at a contemporary gallery
wearing your cuff links and the fancy suit
your father bought you right before
he died and flirting,
actually flirting with someone very cute.

And Dad would say to never get too high or too low.
It's true last Friday walking through
the resplendant crowd on Delmar
for just a moment I felt
as if I were truly the shit and so many
people wanted to hook up with me
but then there was my destitute homeless writer buddy
looking at me with disgust—I deserved it—
and I sadly went down on back home
recalling my many blunders and mistakes.
Nothing's forever. Well, maybe some things are.
I think Ativan and the grace of God are in cahoots.

MY FRIENDS, THE SHORT VERSION

I'm feeling a bit
transdiscursive today—even as
I'm slightly sad and forlorn
that Adam the Jeweler refused
to bump fists with me at Starbucks—
and I'm thinking of popping in
two or three more Ativan
just to chase the devil away
and take me from this wretched judgment.

It all comes back to Livingston
and Lesbia, and how
I have been cursed and cured and delivered
and then died—on medicine—
and said such stupid and erratic stuff
and gone around making
friends with everyone
and trying to present as if I were glad
when the truth is that I suspect that
someone gave me a terrible dose.

Matthew Freeman is a poet from Missouri who writes about his recovery from schizophrenia and addiction and his time spent at Parkview Place and how those facts relate to power, class, and theory. This is his eighth book. He holds an MFA from the University of Missouri-Saint Louis.

www.ingramcontent.com/pod-product-compliance
Lightning Source LLC
Chambersburg PA
CBHW060612080526
44585CB00013B/797